The Housewife's
Guide to:

the PRACTICAL
STRIPTEASE

The Housewife's Guide to the Practical Striptease

copyright 2007
Author: Miyoko Fujimori
Editor: Jeff Rifkin
Illustrations and Graphic Design: Eric Marchbanks

Published by Indulgent Press, Inc.
5699 Kanan Rd, Suite 430
Agoura Hills, CA 91301
www.indulgentpress.com

Table of Contents

Chapter

1

THE FANTASY

The Fantasy

The room is a dark cave, lit only by blinking neon signs and strobing black lights. The fog machine releases a magnificent cloud of smoke which adorns the stage like a velvet cloak. As the smoke begins to fade, the figure of a woman emerges. She's a goddess, perfect in every way, and she's about to get naked.

No wonder he's drooling like a kid in a candy store! Housewives can't compete with an image like this if we hired a crew to build the stage and apply the makeup. If we had the time to shave our bikini lines, glue on false eyelashes, and dedicate an entire 10 minutes to the sole purpose of slowly undressing, we might accept the challenge. But in the last 12 hours we've driven the kids to school, sat through soccer practice, cleaned the house, folded laundry, and fed our families a well-balanced meal. All of this, in addition to a long day at work. The last thing on our minds is competing with a fantasy! But if he looked at you the way he looks at them, you might start to change your perspective.

YOU are reading this book, so you have made an effort towards nurturing your sexuality. Congratulations, YOU are already an incredibly sexy woman! Even if you feel like you lack the ability to do this, you've started on the right track! The fact that you are interested in stripping for your partner is an amazing testament to your relationship, and your self-confidence. It won't take much from here, just a few tweaks and some fine-tuning, and you'll dance like a pro in no time! WARNING! DON'T just read this book and drag him off for his first striptease! You will need to plan, practice, and get comfortable with the moves.

Why Men Love Strippers

Something happens to a man when he enters into the abyss of a strip club. Perhaps he's inhaling too much smoke, or maybe every single boyhood fantasy rushes into his thoughts, clouding his mind from determining what is real and what isn't. Whatever the case, the effect is an evening of albeit shallow, bliss.....

What do Strippers do to make men spew out $20 bills like an ATM machine? What is so magical about the thick layer of make-up, false eyelashes and loud music? Is it simply a combination of the elements that makes these women seem flawless? Is that what men really want, flawless women? Don't they know the boobs are fake? DO they really believe that she's paying her way through medical school? Don't they realize that these women probably have screaming kids at home, and only have sex once or twice a week, just like the rest of us? Even if they knew the truth, they wouldn't care. For this moment, they feel as though they are wanted. During the five minutes they spend with her, they are allowed to be turned on.

Strippers are symbols of sexual freedom, for both genders. Men are allowed to talk openly about sex, without fear of offending them. Women are allowed to be naked, without implying that sex will follow.

It is a business transaction. Men know they are paying for a false sense of affection, and it's OKAY with them. They will spend $20, $40, $100 for a few moments of sweaty flesh bumping and grinding over their laps. They love the tease. They adore the idea of what will never happen, and they are willing to pay well for it. Because when they leave, they will never have to speak to that woman ever again. They will never see her in the light, never know that she didn't look exactly as they remember her. She will never nag him to pick up his dirty clothes, wash dishes or take care of the kids. She will never get angry at him for looking at another woman, not even a naked one. She won't care that he thinks of someone else while she is dancing for him. She won't reject him. She won't point out his faults. She won't expect a phone call the next morning. In fact, she won't care if she NEVER SEES HIM AGAIN. She'll only provide him with the service they've agreed upon.

As wives and mothers, we are often unable to simply enjoy the physical aspect of our sexuality. We are so wrapped up in our day-to-day duties, and our relationships, that we can hardly begin to think of spreading our legs for the person we feel is responsible for it all. Some of you may be thinking, "I'm not gonna strip for him, I barely want to have sex with him!" We THINK we have to like our husbands to have sex with them. But we don't! Put your mop and your gripes aside and look at him as a piece of meat for 20 minutes!

In stripping, you may find a safe place to communicate feelings of resentment or neglect. Wives often feel like they are not desired sexually by their husbands. Husbands often feel as though they don't get enough attention. Yet rarely do we verbalize these feelings. In this simple act of courtship, you can bridge the gap and begin to talk to each other without words. Sometimes all you need are a few grunts and moans to set things straight!

So...

How do we Compete?

⑤

We beat them at their own game! Strippers will never have the one thing we are overflowing in.... experience. We know what makes his toes curl. In fact, we know every inch of his body, and we know what to do with it. He already loves you, so top that off with an erotic striptease, and he'll be putty in your hands. This will be the best dance he's ever had(ahem; not that he's ever had one before...)because his odds of scoring with you are 100% better! His fantasies can really run wild. He's got memories of past lusty nights with you to replay in his mind. And guess what, you can use them too! Whisper dirty words to describe a great night of sex you've had. What did you do? Did he try something different that made you scream? Tell him how it felt..... with AS MUCH DETAIL AS POSSIBLE!

Why we Love to Strip

What's the big deal about getting naked? Will it really change your life? Women's lives can be changed forever once they've experienced the empowerment from taking off their clothes. It is not the naked body, but rather the clothing in our society that has been sexualized over the centuries. It is the fabric draped over our bodies that causes us to wonder and fantasize about what lies beneath. Everything from the toe cleavage in our shoes, to the separation between the buttons on a blouse are targets of sexual response. A clever plan fueled by a multi-billion dollar fashion empire.

Shedding these layers frees us from the confines of what our daily uniforms impose. Our business suits represent an unemotional, static person who sacrifices her sensuality for her power. The mommy sweatsuit screams, "sexually unavailable." And forget about getting some if you're sporting a fast food uniform.... Releasing yourself from the hems and stitches of your clothing allows you to discover your human instincts, primal needs, and carnal desires.

Once our clothes hit the floor we are free to feel and be anyone we want to be! We can be a trampy slut, a graceful goddess, or a shy schoolgirl. We can feel as sensual about our bodies as we want to, and do it without consequence. We can finally celebrate our bodies and relish every luscious curve. Whether you strip for someone or alone in your room, make a commitment to empower yourself. Paying respect to our spiritual temple not only ignites our sexual passions but also rejuvenates our self worth and inner spirit.

⑧

So let's get started!

Choosing your Attire

Preparation is a good way to get you into the mood! Try on different nighties, skirts, lingerie, stockings, or themed outfits and move around in front of a mirror. Dance to music that inspires you....whether it is slow and seductive, or upbeat and funky! Run your hands over your body, swish your skirt from side to side. Begin to find the person you want to be.

Shower, primp and shave. Splash on some perfume, or edible body dust to tempt his senses.

Strippers Speak out!

What are your Favorite scents and powders?

"Body sprays from Victoria's Secret! Especially the vanilla or pear berry."

"Kama Sutra Honey Dust! I can dust it all over, even between my legs to keep my body feeling sweet and fresh. (and you can lick it off too!)"

"Bath and Body Works lotions."

"Why can't I just strip in whatever I'm wearing?" While spur of the moment stripping is a magnificent thing, I'm assuming that most of you are doing this for the first time and want to plan a spectacular event! So trust me on this– you will need to prepare at least a little... So, what do you wear?

Unleash your desires by playing the naughty little school girl inside of you! Or maybe you'd prefer to be the lady in charge and cuff your mate to the bed post? Whether you decide to create a theme, or just strip in his favorite shirt, your attire should reflect the personality you want to bring to your "stage."

Lesson #1

Play Pretend!

Here are some of our favorites:

School girls, or anything related (ie: plaid skirts, cheerleader skirts, pig tails, ruffled socks and heels)

Tough Girls– law enforcement, cowgirls, firefighters, business suits, mechanics, and of course, a Dominatrix.

Movie Sex pots! Kim Bassinger a la 9-1/2 wks (silk slip, thigh-high stockings, and of course, a hat!) Risky business (white button-up man's shirt, undies and socks) Moulin Rouge (bustiers, corsets, bodices, feather boas, hats, or scarves, anything glamourous...)

Stripper's Shoes

Where do you find those platform patent leather stiletto heels? If you live near a major metropolitan area, chances are that you can find a stripper store for some "slut gear." If not, search online for "stripper shoes" and several good places will pop up! They're not as difficult to walk in as they look. The platform styles are really quite comfortable, and you won't be wearing them for long!

Getting your guy to strip?

Here are some suggestions
for him!

Tough Guys– Cowboys, cops,
firefighters, and construction
workers get our panties in a
bunch!

Men In Uniform– A man in
uniform gets me going any
day of the week!

⑭

Dressing in Drag- This only works if you're turned on by
the sight of him in women's clothing, or if it was his humor
that made you marry him... proceed with caution!

TIP!!

Paint your Toe Nails! In my early days as a stripper it took a
long time for me to figure this out. Toes and feet can be incredibly sexy! We tend to forget about the little details, so be sure to
pay attention to them. Even if they are just painted clear, you'll
notice an added boost of self-esteem by spoiling your piggies with
some pampering. And self-confidence = sexy!

Personal Hygiene

To Shave or Not to Shave? Most people seem to have a fascination with a hairless, or at least, well-groomed, pubic area these days. Whether this is what you prefer, or not, it can be an exciting surprise for your mate when the final pieces of clothing come off! Be sure to shave carefully, your assets are valuable!

The "landing strip" has been named for it's long rectangular shape. To achieve this look, you'll want to remove the hair from the sides of your bikini line, and the outer labia. The rectangle of hair would normally stop just above the clitoris, but you can also leave some around the "lips" to frame the inner labia. Most dancers continue the shave all the way around to the anus, but this is of course at your discretion. You can lift your leg up on a toilet seat, or shower seat to help you get underneath your bottom. Feel for stray hairs with your fingers, or use a mirror to get a perfect trim. Triangular cuts are more natural looking, diamond trims put a sparkle in his eye, and arrows are a great way to point him in the right direction!

Try some special shapes for a festive holiday "doo!" Hearts for Valentine's Day, a four-leaf clover for St Patty's,

Strippers Speak out!

Most exotic dancers have battled with ingrown hairs, and razor burn from shaving. What are their secrets?

"Mach 3 Razor & lots of shaving cream."

"Shave in the direction of the hair."

"Get a professional waxing!"

"Tweeze the bikini line."

"Use Tend Skin during and after shaving."

"Nair, just don't get it too close to the inner labia."

"Nads, a great self waxing product that works!"

"Get laser hair removal and be done with it forever!"

An added bonus! Shaving or waxing your genital area can heighten your sensitivity! If you don't want to go all the way, you can still grab some scissors and a comb, and give that kitty a trim! We don't call it carpet munching for nothing!

Choosing the MUSIC

"Am I sexy now?"

Juliette Lewis was incredibly hot when she so eloquently spoke those words in Natural Born Killers. You remember the scene.... she seduces the young boy at the gas station, climbs onto the red sportscar and commands him to "Go Down." Right on sister! Of course, then she killed him.... but the point is, the song that played in the background will forever be a sexy song to strip by. There are several songs that inspire the rebel woman in us. Pick a song that makes you touch yourself, makes you melt, makes you horny. Turn it on and play it loud.

Lesson
#2

Play it Loud
and
get lost in the music!

Does it have to be loud ?

Yes! You are creating an atmosphere. The sound of your heels on a carpet or vinyl floor completely ruin the vibe. It's pretty hard to feel glamourous when you are reminded that you are as far from a stage as possible. Your man probably won't notice. But, you'll hear everything from your heart beating (more like racing), to the sound of your panties hitting the floor. These are the last things we should be thinking about! You should be completely engaged in yourself and your husband!

DO A THEME SHOW!

Don't be disappointed if your honey doesn't get it. I'm sure that less than 10% of the guys who saw me perform even knew what I was dancing to, let alone made a connection to the outfit I was wearing. Your man may not understand the reference between your music choice and the outfit, but you will.

Music to Strip By

There are so many tunes that get the juices flowing. So much of the 80's hair band music was a love letter to strippers and it makes you want to "Take it off!" as the song goes.... AC/DC, Motley Crue, White Snake, Warrant, Def Leopard, The Cult, U2, and Lenny Kravitz, give you that naughty feeling, and the energy to do something about it. Bands like White Zombie, Nine Inch Nails, Marilyn Manson scream of sexuality in its most primal form. Hip-hop, Rap and R&B singers have been performing songs about strippers for years. Then there's Prince, need I say more? If fast songs aren't your cup of tea, just about anything from performers like Sade, Dead Can Dance, Enigma, Portishead and Moby with their sultry vibes and eclectic sounds, will make your hips sway and your hair come down. You can cue up one song for the main course and let the rest of the album play as background for dessert!

Here are some examples of songs to accompany themed outfits or costumes. These songs make you feel like you are on a stage. Many of them have an introduction. Wait for the beats that really hit for your grand entrance!

School girls. etc.
"Hot for Teacher"
"Girls, Girls, Girls..."
"Smoking in the Boys' Room"
    Motley Crue
"Shoot and Ladders"
    Korn
"I want candy"
    Bow Wow Wow
"Just a girl"
    No Doubt

Jungle or Animal Prints
"Wild Child"
    W.A.S.P.
"Welcome to the Jungle"
    Guns and Roses
"The Animal"
    Steve Vai
"Jungle Boogie"
    Kool & the Gang
"Black Cat"
    Janet Jackson

TIP!!

Have the stereo cued up and ready to go, then leave the remote control in his favorite spot with a note that reads, "Play me..." (You may need to include the words, "Push play," to ensure that there is no room for error at this point. They are, afterall, still men.) Then have another sexy album ready to play once things start to heat up. If you're computer savvy, you can compile a list of songs and burn your own disc!

Nurse or Doctor
"Dr Feelgood"
    Motley Crue
"Clean my wounds"
    Corrosion of Conformity
"Time to get Ill"
    Beastie Boys

Firewoman

"Red Hot"
   Motley Crue
"Sleep Now in the Fire"
   Rage against the machine
"Fire Woman"
   The Cult
"Fan the Fire"
"Serpentine Fire"
   Earth, Wind, & Fire
"On Fire"
   Lloyd Banks
"Full of Fire"
   Al Green
"The Unforgettable Fire"
   U2

Cowgirls

"Cowboy"
   Kid Rock
"Cowboys from Hell"
   Pantera
"Where Have all the Cowboys Gone?"
   Paula Cole
"Cowboys"
   Portishead
"Cowboys and Cowgirls"
   The Wiggles
   (oops! This one only works as a joke!)
& of course, any country western song will do...

Got some of your own ideas? If you have your own original outfits or funky feelings, go online to a music download program and search for your title! You'll have a song to match that costume in no time!

Police Officer

"Smoked Pork"
   Body Count
"Killing in the name"
"Fistful of Steel"
   Rage against the machine
"Bad Boys"
   Inner Circle
"I shot the Sheriff"
   Bob Marley
"Shoot to Thrill"
   AC/DC

Sexy Soundtrack Music

"You Can Leave Your Hat On"
   Joe Cocker (9 1/2 weeks)
"Feelin' Love "
   Paula Cole (City of Angels)
"Sweet Jane"
   Cowboy Junkies (Natural Born Killers)
"Mouth"
   Bush (An American Werewolf in Paris)
"In your eyes"
   Peter Gabriel (Say Anything)
"Woman in Chains"
   Tears for Fears (Boxing Helena)
"Lady Marmalade"
   Christina Aguilera (Moulin Rouge)

Lighting

Lighting is Everything! Strippers have an amazing aura of angelic perfection when on stage, and it's not because they are... trust me... You won't feel particularly sexy if you are obsessing over every little butt zit, or razor bump in your newly shaven bikini line, so let's keep those lights to a minimum. You want them to see the goods, but you also need to create an atmosphere. You can't do that if you're getting slapped in the face with too much of your own reality! We don't all have strobe lights and fog machines installed in our bedrooms. If you happen to have them, great! For the rest of us, you'll need to get a little more creative. Candlelight is a magnificent backdrop for your naked flesh. Just be careful not to start any fires other than the ones in their pants! Flashlights can be extremely erotic! Let your lover flash the light wherever he wants. Give him a few flashlights to spotlight your best assets! If you can't manage any of those, get a low watt bulb in your lamp, or use your dimmer and create a stage for yourself!

Props

"But I don't have any props!" I'm not talking about a ring of fire or an oversized champagne glass! Props can include things that you can "play" with during your show. A pair of eyeglasses, a boa, handcuffs, a crop whip... Props will help complete your outfit and keep you busy. Furniture can also be considered props in this case. You can and should use a chair, bed, or any other piece of stable furniture to dance on or around. Why? Because although HE may not get bored of seeing you move your body in one place, YOU will! Are you hearing a theme here? You need to entertain yourself in order to entertain him! The key to any good strip tease is this: You are as interesting as you feel.

Try to position yourself in a room where there is a wall, couch, or chair and something to lean on. Some floor space for floorwork is a must, and a doorway if possible.

Lesson #3

The key to any good striptease is this: You are as interesting as you feel

Chapter

3

THE MOVES

The MOVES

You've seen strippers doing some weird thing with their legs that make you think they are tying them in knots. What makes us watch this pretzel leg move like we're being hypnotized?

The idea behind the crossing and uncrossing of the legs "move" has been around for decades. Sharon Stone did it best in the scene that made her unforgettable. It's a tease. Did you see it? You most likely rented it and rewound it until you thought you had! (Believe me when I tell you that HE DID! He put that VCR on slow motion until he had the frame captured just right and paused it to stare at the forbidden mound of downy fur between her legs) The idea was to tease. Hence, Strip tease....

Lesson
#4
Tease them
relentlessly!

There are a lot of ways to draw his attention to what you want him to see... Skirts are the epitome of this idea. They move on their own, with the help of the slightest sway on our part. When we sit or bend over, they rise... what a wonderful invention. Skirts can be manipulated manually as well. We can raise them, and lower them willfully. Skirts that are free to hang while panties slowly slide down soft thighs, can be enough to send him over the edge! Dance with them around your mid-thighs for awhile. Leave them dangling there, letting your lover's mind run wild waiting for them to finally come off completely. The sight of your lowered panties is a blaring signal that your vagina is exposed.

• • • • • • • • • • • • • • • • • •

Easy access! Other primates are not bipedal, they walk on all fours leaving their genitals in the perfect alignment for intercourse, but not humans. We have concealed our signs of mating availability and sexual arousal. Men are required to woo, anticipate, and engage in extended foreplay before they are even allowed the opportunity to penetrate us. This green light to your pot of gold is rarely a signal in the world of diapers and dishes, so give him a treat! He deserves it!

The Walk,
The Hair Toss,
and The Look

Up against a wall

Put your face up against the wall with your rear facing your man. Lean into the wall pressing your cheek to it. With your legs open, lift your skirt, dress, or slip, and slide a hand over your buns! Bend forward all the way if you're flexible enough and run your hand slowly up the outside of your leg. play with your panties, or G-string. Pull them down, or over to one side exposing your delicate flower.

Bend over

Just as its name implies, bend over and flaunt the goods. Wave your ass in front of their face, parade your coochy around the room, back it up to their chair.... however you present your entrance to ecstasy, do it with the knowledge that they are hypnotized by the thought of diving into your oasis.

Spank me Facing a wall, chair, window, or even a refrigerator, bend forward and present your ass to your audience, fall to one side and look up from behind your hair.

Drop and Spread 'em

Stand with your back to the wall, doorway, or pole (if you've got it) with your legs a bit more than hip distance apart. Slowly begin to squat down, opening your legs as you go. Leaning more to one side or the other once you've dropped down will help you better your balance.

(30)

The treasure between your legs isn't the only thing you can tease them with. Nipples are the golden jewels of the upper body. Delicately draped slips over a naked set of breasts are incredibly sexy. Camisoles and bustiers are great tools for stripping because they accentuate the breasts. Peek-a-boo bras and teddies provide the same effect and give you the thrill of wearing naughty lingerie!

Lacy bras, or plain white tank tops, are perfect for playing, and beg to be taken off.

Pull down on one side, or lift up just enough to see the lower half of the breast, but not all. Straps seem to conveniently fall off of shoulders revealing the slope of your bosom.... let them. Don't take the clothes off too soon, let them play along with you.

Breast squeeze

Kneel on both knees and then sit back onto your feet, then reach under your breasts and lift them in an upward squeezing motion. If you can lick a nipple, go for it! If this pose is too difficult to do you can also straddle a chair, or sit on your ass with your legs spread out in front of you (knees bent) while doing the breast squeeze.

The walk

Strippers have a distinct walk. Unlike the power stride of supermodels, strippers have a deliberate drag to their feet. Walk to your audience as though you're walking on a tight rope. Place one foot in front of the other in a straight line. Start slowly, chest out, with your head held high. Step forward and firmly plant one foot as you drag your other foot behind you, leaving the top part of your toes on the floor for as long as possible. Then pull it through as you plant it firmly on the floor repeating the same motion with the other foot. Once you get the technique down, you can speed it up or slow it down. Add a sway to your stride by swinging your hips and bending your knees.

There is a reason that long hair is sexy! Tossing your locks around while you are dancing is a total stripper move. But only if you do it the right way. (Yes, there is a wrong way.) Make sure that you relax your neck and swirl your head all the way around. It should feel as though you are stretching it out. Your hair will follow naturally. If you try to swing your hair, it'll end up looking like a bad dance from the 80's. You can swing your head gently from side to side, using your hair to play peek-a-boo with your eyes.

Incorporate the hair toss whenever you can, it works best when your body is turning at the same time. Turning around a chair, pole, or through a doorway, is a great time to throw around those locks. Practice by standing up straight, place one foot in front of you and begin to pivot on your feet. As you step forward, tilt your head to the same side as the foot you have put forward and roll your head in the same direction as you are turning. Practice, practice, practice!

You can shake it aggressively in a wild display of your inner tigress, or you can flip your head as you come up from a bent over position. However you use your hair to tempt, make sure it's sensuous and genuine. (Rolling the eyes while flipping the hair doesn't quite cut it!) Short hair is equally sexy, it just doesn't get the same trajectory! So instead of using your hair, pay attention to the slope of your neck.

Play with a scarf, tie, or string of pearls to dangle over your vampire's delight!

Smile: A smile can easily melt your man of steel. Knowing that you are enjoying what you are doing is a huge turn on. Seeing you smile also creates intimacy.

The Eyes: They say that the eyes are the window to the soul. An intense stare will bring them to their knees! You can do so much with your eyes. Remember staring down your friends as a kid? Same concept, but this time, you can't lose! Don't let them make you feel uncomfortable. YOU are in control. YOU decide what they will have the priviledge of touching. You have the power, and it feels good!

Penetrate them with your gaze. Make them know how much they want you. Glide your finger over your teeth as though you are going to stick it in your mouth and suck on it, but don't. You're a woman, not a baby.

Strippers Speak out!

Most dancers who make good money will tell you that the secret to a good dance is eye contact. "If you can look a guy in the face and stare him down, you've got him. He'll keep paying until he's broke!"

Let your fingers fall to touch yourself whereever your little heart desires. (Tasting yourself afterward may make them blow their wad so be careful-- they are putty in your hands at this point!)

(36)

Your vagina is suffocating! Let her breathe sister! Ever realized how much time we spend keeping our legs closed each day? Just open them and you'll find out. Just opening our legs while we bathe in a hot bubble bath or as we watch TV in our bedrooms at night can bring us closer to our erotic center. Open your legs every now and then, and you'll learn to pay homage to your inner sex kitten!

Floor Work

The hard part of floor work is getting down there gracefully. Once you master this move, you'll move from wall to floor to chair easily. Start by standing, legs more than shoulder length apart. Assuming you are right handed, turn the right foot inward and bend the same leg bringing your knee to the floor. 1. You'll be in a marriage proposal position for a split second as you lean backward placing your right hand on the floor about one foot behind you. Shift your weight backward as you move your pelvis forward in a backbend motion. 2. Swing your right foot in a circular motion inward and out, sitting your ass on the floor. Open your left leg out and keep it bent. Now that you have landed, you can sit with your legs bent and spread open in front of you. This is a great time to use your eyes, touch yourself or lay on the floor for the next move!

3

I know this seems overwhelming! But if you take this move one step at a time and practice it, it'll be a piece of cake!

Bang Me!

Lay back on your elbows and bring your legs up toward your chest. (yes, like you're giving birth!) You can open them up in an even spread, rock them from side to side, pump them as though you are being ravished, or bend them alternately and bicycle them down.

㊳

Bicycle

To bicycle them down.... slowly glide feet (or heels) together and alternate them, toes pointed in a bicycle motion. As you lower your head to the floor and arch your back. You can wrap your arms around your chest, or caress your breasts and neck in this position.

Now that you are flat on the floor, what next?

Come and Get it!

Turn over to your stomach, begin to come up on all fours, raising your ass first. Stop for a moment with your ass in the air, legs spread, leaving your cheek on the floor. Push your ass in the air, as you lower your stomach towards the ground. This may take a little flexibility, but with practice, you'll get it down. Look around the side of your hips and run your hands through your legs to touch yourself again. Oh yeah! You're smokin' mama!

Cum hither

Continue laying with your cheek on the ground and with your ass still raised in the air, crawl backwards to your man. Before you reach him, crawl away!

Add a Little Yoga!

Stretching your body through Yoga invites healing, flexibility, and change. Baddha Konasana, or cobbler's pose, promotes good health in the urinary tract and reproductive organs and is also known for aiding in pregnancy and menstrual symptoms. Check out books on Yoga at your local library, join a class, or search online to make sure you're doing it properly.

Cat Crawl

On your hands and knees take long strides in an almost sluggish way, letting your hair fall into your eyes. Let your back sink into your shoulders, and your hips move naturally with the motion of the crawl. A shy smile, or a seductive purr (ONLY if you can pull it off!) is a sexy addition to this submissive move.

Run Away Kitty!

This crawl can also be performed facing away from your man! Turn around to peek and watch him watching you. Be sure to play the part! You know he's tempted to chase after you and drag you back, swing that ass like it's a bone for a dog!

Lap Dancing

If you decide to incorporate a lap dance (which I highly recommend!) into your performance, set the ground rules first! Can they touch? Or will you tie their hands behind their back? Enforcing someone else's self-control can be tons of fun especially when you make it nearly impossible for them to keep their hands (and tongues) to themselves!

Begin by dancing around or in front of them and gradually make your way to their lap.

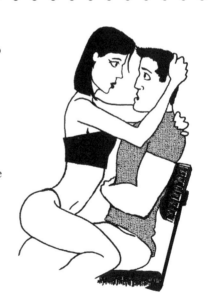

Meow!

Climb onto their lap like a feline, or straddle one or both of their legs, and bring your face close enough for them to feel your breath.

A kiss

Get your lips danger-ously close, but don't kiss. Embrace them with your arms and delicately run your fingers through their hair. Nibble on their ears, lightly kiss their neck. Lick their lips, but don't allow them to lick back.

Face Rub

Rub your face, neck, and chest on his face, building an intimate bond between you. Lower your head onto his lap and rub your cheek on his growing bulge. Sit down between his legs and lick him over his pants. Make sure to look him in the eyes!

The Grind

When you're ready for things to progress, grind, rub or go down! "What is grinding?" It's that thing you did in high school. The "safe sex", over the clothes, rubbing of your pubic areas that made you both crazy with lust! Grind him facing forward, grind him with your back to him. Reach between your legs and stroke him with your hand. Watch out if he's got jeans on. Grinding can hurt! Especially with your newly shaven bikini line.

"Are all lap dances like this?"

Definitely not! Dancers do as little as possible for that $20 bill. Most dancers only get as close as they need to when performing a lap or table dance. In many cities they are required to be as far as 6ft away. Local law enforcement won't allow contact of gential areas, touching of themselves, or their patrons. Your man has probably NEVER had a dance like the one you're about to give him!

Strippers Speak Out About Lap Dancing

"I can't wait until the song ends. Most lap dances are as long as one song, (that has been cut short, by the way.) I do as little as possible. I just move around in front of them, flash a little cookie and that's it."

"I pretend like I'm into him when I'm facing him. But when I turn around, I make faces at my friends, think about what I have to do the next day."

"I hate to grind, it hurts! But if I do, I'll grind with my hip, my thigh, or my butt instead."

Putting it all together...

So you've practiced each "move," mastered the "hair toss" thing. How do you put it all together to look like one sexy erotic dance? Like anything in life, "practice makes perfect." But, I don't recommend you plan and choreograph a whole song and dance. Spontaneity looks better when you're talking about seduction. Plan it too much, and you'll look like a lame cheerleader. Don't get too into the "production." The purpose is to seduce and entertain the person watching you. So your next move will depend on what they are reacting to. If they are obviously enjoying you in a particular position, play there longer. If it's time to mount your steed, then by all means, get it on girl!

Tip!!

Practice your dance where you'll perform it. This way you'll know how far it is to crawl from the couch to the chair where he'll be waiting. Do a few dress rehearsals before the big night. Get an idea of what your "props" are, and where they are located.

Chapter

4

GETTING YOUR GROOVE ON

Getting your Groove On

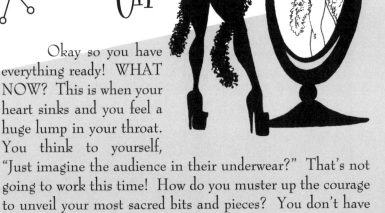

Okay so you have everything ready! WHAT NOW? This is when your heart sinks and you feel a huge lump in your throat. You think to yourself, "Just imagine the audience in their underwear?" That's not going to work this time! How do you muster up the courage to unveil your most sacred bits and pieces? You don't have to...

Courage is what you would need to shed your layers for a room full of strangers. Self-esteem and personal acceptance are what you need to take it all off for the one you love. Unfortunately, these are harder to come by.

"But I hate my body!"

Forget about yourself as the entire body. Think of yourself in pieces. Imagine a camera zoomed in to exactly what you want them to see. The slope of your neck, the bounce in your breast, the sparkle in your eyes. Take the time to appreciate and cherish the parts of your body that you are least impressed with. Getting completely nude creates a forgiving dynamic. When we have removed the facade, the clothing, and eventually the baggage, we have nothing more to hide behind. It is truly liberating. You may be surprised at how much you actually do like your body. Sometimes we just need to be re-introduced.

 ## "Easy for you to say!"

Remember this, there is something incredibly sexy about each one of us. You all have a best feature. Momma always said, "Use what ya got!" It may be those bedroom eyes, a sexy smile, a great ass, or long legs. Focus on it and work it girl!

Strippers Speak out!

"The first time I danced I had no idea what to do. I was a cheerleader in high school, so I choreographed a little routine to 8 counts and practiced it over and over. I wore the sexiest bra and panties I could find. A black bra and black thong panty. I tried to get rid of my full bottom tan lines that day. It didn't work. I wore the only black heels I had.... business heels with a mary jane kind of look. I remember walking onto the stage and doing the first move, but that's it. The rest is a blur. I fell in love with dancing right then and there."

Still Shy?

If you are still too concerned with what your husband is thinking during your erotic serenade, close your eyes, and forget about him. Simply relish in what feels good to you. This will please him more. If all else fails, blindfold him! Do a dance that involves blindfolding him before you lose the clothes. Slowly let him "discover" what you are revealing, with his hands and lips.

Learning to love yourself

Lesson #5 Love yourself !!!

Oddly enough, the more you expose your flaws the more you'll grow to accept them. You may even begin to love them. Men are amazingly visual creatures and can get off on the smallest details. Foot fetishes, ass fetishes, armpits, pubic hair, the way we taste, the way we smell, our ears, our necks, our nipples, our soft belly.... men have adored women for centuries. When Adam ate the forbidden fruit, he began the infinite love affair with the sanctuary known as the female body. Never underestimate the power of the mind.

Beware!

Once you open the door to honest communication, you may be surprised at what you hear. Your man may have an insatiable longing for a particular part of your anatomy, or to try a different sexual act. Remember that this is the man you love and that includes acceptance of things you may not understand. Take it as a compliment and as long as you're willing, move slowly in the direction of his fantasies.

A few ideas to tempt his fetishes...

Foot jobs

If he's into feet, he'll love feeling your freshly painted toes dancing over his throbbing member. Sit on the floor between his legs and use your feet to stroke and gently rub his bulge. Spray some whipped cream or pour chocolate syrup over your toes and let him lick them clean. Or if he's really into your feet, wear a pair of stiletto boots during your striptease and for the grand finale, take them off and let him smell the sweaty leather scent of your flesh.

Food fetish?

Make yourself his most decadent meal. Plan a Naked Buffet Night and let him devour every course off of your delicious flesh. Be sure to give yourself a long hot bath to wash away any traces of perfumes and lotions (and the funk from your long hard day at work!) You may want to indulge this fetish in a place that is easy to clean up. Do it in the kitchen, or lay down some plastic or an old sheet in your dining room, or bedroom. Or get a hotel room for the night and let someone else clean up the mess!

Sexy foods like succulent berries, chocolate sauce, and champagne are a guaranteed hit! You can use whipped cream to get the berries to stick to your skin long enough for him to eat them off. If you want to feed him dinner, try sushi placed strategically in all the right areas of your body. Cold noodle salads or long pastas make a mess when you feed him with your toes! WE DON'T RECOMMEND a steak dinner, or soups! These foods may fill his gut, but they won't get you any action! Almost any food can be sexy if presented or shared the right way. Feed him with your mouth, your breasts, your thighs, any part of your body! Be creative, and you'll have a blast!

That's it !

Rinse and repeat! We hope that the first striptease will lead to many more nights of sensual dancing and spontaneous lap dances.

Most likely you will have turned him on long before you began to undress. Just the thought of what is to come, is enough to have him "saying your name" for weeks! Self-confidence is one of the top "most attractive" qualities to both sexes, and definitely makes for better lovemaking. So...

Whatever happens once the lights dim and the music starts is simply icing on the cake! So practice a little in the mirror, scope out the furniture in your room of choice, turn down the lights, turn up the tunes, and a plan lusty night for you and your man!

A New Perspective

Now that you have experienced the art of the striptease, practice often! Dance in your bedroom at night. Dance while you clean the house! Welcome this new woman with open arms and embrace this new perspective of your body. Relish in this new attitude. You are a magnificent woman, honor her.

It will more than likely take a few performances for you to feel like a pro. It took me four months of dancing three nights a week to finally find my niche. You may be surprised to discover your inner sex kitten is really a dirty-talking slut! You may get the urge to moan, or scream. Let it go! Dancing as a form of self expression has been around since early man, so don't worry about what he'll think. Trust me, he's gonna love meeting the sex goddess you've been keeping locked up inside.

Quick Guide

Lesson #1 – Play pretend!

Lesson #2 – Play music loud and get lost in the moment! Create a stage for yourself.

Lesson #3 – The key to any good striptease is this: You are as interesting as you feel. Choose music, props, and and an outfit that inspire you.

Lesson #4 – Tease them relentlessly! Don't take your clothes off too soon let them play along with you! The most important thing? Eye Contact....

Lesson #5 – Love yourself! You are a magnificent woman, honor her.

What Not To Do For Your First Time...

1. **Don't** be too serious about yourself. You're not doing a Broadway show! Just use what makes YOU sexy and you'll have him exactly where you want him.

2. **Don't** get on top of unsteady furniture! Don't climb on tables, or chairs that can't handle the weight, or may topple over. This will definitely cut your striptease short.

3. **Don't** get a haircut, wax, laser, or a serious facial right before your big debut. If you are familiar with these procedures, you already know this. If you want to do something special to pamper yourself and boost your ego before the performance, make sure your body has plenty of time to heal.

4. **Don't** go barefoot on your first performance. I know this may sound a little contradictory to the whole "feet are important" thing, but you should do everything you can to feel as sexy as possible. High heels create a mood. Once you've gotten your stripping persona down, you'll be able to strip in anything and everything, or nothing at all but your self confidence.

5. **Don't** get an outfit that requires work to get undressed. It is difficult to disrobe gracefully. That's why Hollywood skips over the part where their shoes and socks came off! You never see the actors fumbling with panties or boxers around their ankles. Get panties that tie at the sides, or rip-away! Once you get good at it, wear whatever you'd like.

About the Author
cuz you know you wanna know!

Miyoko is the perfect "Strip Coach" for women of today! As a former actress, model, and TV host, she understands the struggles of everyday women to compete with the shallow, fantasy portrayal of women in the media. But as a stay-at-home mommy of two, she balances the scale of domestic mama and sex goddess. So with these two incredibly contradictory and yet complementary personalities, she is able to offer an amazing perspective to the hip, young soccer moms and housewives of this generation.

To find out more about Miyoko, visit

www.indulgentpress.com

A Special Thank You

Abundant thanks to everyone who continually encourages and supports me in life. My adoring husband Jeff, my beautiful children Nina and Jack, my mother Jennifer, and my amazing group of friends and fellow sisters. Without all of you I wouldn't be the woman I am today.

A special thanks to those who helped me in the loving and sometimes tedious creation of this book. Jeff, my partner in work and in life. Eric for the ideas and illustrations, Kelly, Lori, Angela, and other gals for sharing their stories, Patrick for making it real, and all of you for buying it!

To all of the above, thank you for believing in me and this project. I am and will be... forever grateful.

Watch for...

Instructional videos/DVDs so you can learn the Practical Striptease right in your living room!

Private instruction available, check out the website for more info!